Questions lovingly answered by:

_________________ & _________________

How do I love thee? Let me count the ways.
I love thee to the depth and breadth and height
My soul can reach, when feeling out of sight
For the ends of being and ideal grace.
I love thee to the level of every day's
Most quiet need, by sun and candle-light.
I love thee freely, as men strive for right.
I love thee purely, as they turn from praise.
I love thee with the passion put to use
In my old griefs, and with my childhood's faith.
I love thee with a love I seemed to lose
With my lost saints. I love thee with the breath,
Smiles, tears, of all my life; and, if God choose,
I shall but love thee better after death.

— Elizabeth Barrett Browning —

Would you rather have a white or a brown dog?

☐ HER REPLY ☐ HIS REPLY

☐ HIS REPLY ☐ HER REPLY

What was the hardest thing about your relationship?

☐ HER REPLY ☐ HIS REPLY

☐ HIS REPLY ☐ HER REPLY

Why did you take the more difficult path?

☐ HER REPLY ☐ HIS REPLY

☐ HIS REPLY ☐ HER REPLY

What causes you to get tired?

☐ HER REPLY ☐ HIS REPLY

☐ HIS REPLY ☐ HER REPLY

What do you think is the most important thing to remember?

☐ HER REPLY ☐ HIS REPLY

☐ HIS REPLY ☐ HER REPLY

If you could have one dream job in your life, what would it be and why?

☐ HER REPLY ☐ HIS REPLY

☐ HIS REPLY ☐ HER REPLY

What is the one thing that bugs you about fast food today?

☐ HER REPLY ☐ HIS REPLY   ☐ HIS REPLY ☐ HER REPLY

What was the book that you did enjoy that you thought you would never find the time to read?

☐ HER REPLY ☐ HIS REPLY   ☐ HIS REPLY ☐ HER REPLY

Would you rather wear __________ or __________?
Why?

☐ HER REPLY ☐ HIS REPLY   ☐ HIS REPLY ☐ HER REPLY

List of things that are a great test of the strength of a champion

☐ HER REPLY ☐ HIS REPLY   ☐ HIS REPLY ☐ HER REPLY

What did you find?

☐ HER REPLY ☐ HIS REPLY   ☐ HIS REPLY ☐ HER REPLY

List of things that cost you money

☐ HER REPLY ☐ HIS REPLY   ☐ HIS REPLY ☐ HER REPLY

Have you ever considered what life would be like if you were able to see things from the inside out?

☐ HER REPLY ☐ HIS REPLY   ☐ HIS REPLY ☐ HER REPLY

What is the meaning of your name? Are you happy with it? Why?

☐ HER REPLY ☐ HIS REPLY   ☐ HIS REPLY ☐ HER REPLY

What would you be willing to sacrifice for your new preferences?

☐ HER REPLY ☐ HIS REPLY

____

____

____

____

____

____

____

____

☐ HIS REPLY ☐ HER REPLY

____

____

____

____

____

____

____

____

List of things that can never stop

☐ HER REPLY ☐ HIS REPLY

____

____

____

____

____

____

☐ HIS REPLY ☐ HER REPLY

____

____

____

____

____

____

What's your relationship like now?

☐ HER REPLY ☐ HIS REPLY

☐ HIS REPLY ☐ HER REPLY

What is the perfect first kiss?

☐ HER REPLY ☐ HIS REPLY

☐ HIS REPLY ☐ HER REPLY

List of things that scare you

☐ HER REPLY ☐ HIS REPLY

☐ HIS REPLY ☐ HER REPLY

If the opportunity came up to team up with a supervillain of your choice, who would it be and why?

☐ HER REPLY ☐ HIS REPLY

☐ HIS REPLY ☐ HER REPLY

What is a good thing that happened to you today?

☐ HER REPLY ☐ HIS REPLY

☐ HIS REPLY ☐ HER REPLY

List of things that matter

☐ HER REPLY ☐ HIS REPLY

☐ HIS REPLY ☐ HER REPLY

How does your child feel about you when you're not there?

☐ HER REPLY ☐ HIS REPLY

☐ HIS REPLY ☐ HER REPLY

What is the one thing that could make you feel less depressed and more like yourself?

☐ HER REPLY ☐ HIS REPLY

☐ HIS REPLY ☐ HER REPLY

What's your first reaction when you see a new car you like?

☐ HER REPLY ☐ HIS REPLY

☐ HIS REPLY ☐ HER REPLY

If you could only play one video game, what would it be?

☐ HER REPLY ☐ HIS REPLY

☐ HIS REPLY ☐ HER REPLY

If you had to choose one thing, what would you want as a parting gift from your former colleague?

☐ HER REPLY ☐ HIS REPLY

☐ HIS REPLY ☐ HER REPLY

What is the best thing you did for your team?

☐ HER REPLY ☐ HIS REPLY

☐ HIS REPLY ☐ HER REPLY

Would you rather not think about it?

☐ HER REPLY ☐ HIS REPLY

☐ HIS REPLY ☐ HER REPLY

What is the one thing your technique hasn't changed?

☐ HER REPLY ☐ HIS REPLY

☐ HIS REPLY ☐ HER REPLY

Tell us a story or a quote about a person you admire and why.

☐ HER REPLY ☐ HIS REPLY   ☐ HIS REPLY ☐ HER REPLY

Rewrite the 12 Days of Christmas with the gifts that you actually want to receive.

☐ HER REPLY ☐ HIS REPLY   ☐ HIS REPLY ☐ HER REPLY

If you could have 3 wishes, what would they be?

☐ HER REPLY ☐ HIS REPLY

☐ HIS REPLY ☐ HER REPLY

Do you enjoy the smell of flowers? Why?

☐ HER REPLY ☐ HIS REPLY

☐ HIS REPLY ☐ HER REPLY

Do you love being around people? Why?

☐ HER REPLY ☐ HIS REPLY   ☐ HIS REPLY ☐ HER REPLY

_______________________________   _______________________________
_______________________________   _______________________________
_______________________________   _______________________________
_______________________________   _______________________________
_______________________________   _______________________________
_______________________________   _______________________________
_______________________________   _______________________________
_______________________________   _______________________________
_______________________________   _______________________________

What's your best trait?

☐ HER REPLY ☐ HIS REPLY   ☐ HIS REPLY ☐ HER REPLY

_______________________________   _______________________________
_______________________________   _______________________________
_______________________________   _______________________________
_______________________________   _______________________________
_______________________________   _______________________________
_______________________________   _______________________________
_______________________________   _______________________________

What is your daily routine like?

☐ HER REPLY ☐ HIS REPLY   ☐ HIS REPLY ☐ HER REPLY

Where do your kids go to school?

☐ HER REPLY ☐ HIS REPLY   ☐ HIS REPLY ☐ HER REPLY

What is your least favorite advice you've ever received?

☐ HER REPLY ☐ HIS REPLY   ☐ HIS REPLY ☐ HER REPLY

Have you ever felt love that was undeniable? Why?

☐ HER REPLY ☐ HIS REPLY   ☐ HIS REPLY ☐ HER REPLY

What was the biggest nightmare you've faced?

□ HER REPLY □ HIS REPLY   □ HIS REPLY □ HER REPLY

What's your favorite place to be in a group?

□ HER REPLY □ HIS REPLY   □ HIS REPLY □ HER REPLY

What do you think has gotten your best in life?

☐ HER REPLY ☐ HIS REPLY   ☐ HIS REPLY ☐ HER REPLY

How do you deal with a man whose sole mission in life is to make you fall off the ledge?

☐ HER REPLY ☐ HIS REPLY   ☐ HIS REPLY ☐ HER REPLY

Do you have a passion for film? Why? Why not?

☐ HER REPLY ☐ HIS REPLY

☐ HIS REPLY ☐ HER REPLY

What does your child like to do when he/she's sad?

☐ HER REPLY ☐ HIS REPLY

☐ HIS REPLY ☐ HER REPLY

If you had to be someone else for 24 hours, who would you choose and why? What would you do?

☐ HER REPLY ☐ HIS REPLY

☐ HIS REPLY ☐ HER REPLY

____

What is your favorite kind of dinner?

☐ HER REPLY ☐ HIS REPLY

☐ HIS REPLY ☐ HER REPLY

____

What is one thing you could change?

☐ HER REPLY   ☐ HIS REPLY

☐ HIS REPLY   ☐ HER REPLY

Would you rather be someone else?

☐ HER REPLY   ☐ HIS REPLY

☐ HIS REPLY   ☐ HER REPLY

What is the worst thing someone has ever said to you?

☐ HER REPLY   ☐ HIS REPLY

☐ HIS REPLY   ☐ HER REPLY

What is a good piece of advice to give someone who's been raised to believe in lies and who is still going through life questioning them?

☐ HER REPLY   ☐ HIS REPLY

☐ HIS REPLY   ☐ HER REPLY

What does your son need the most?

☐ HER REPLY ☐ HIS REPLY

☐ HIS REPLY ☐ HER REPLY

What do children learn about the world in games?

☐ HER REPLY ☐ HIS REPLY

☐ HIS REPLY ☐ HER REPLY

Why do you think you can make friends?

☐ HER REPLY ☐ HIS REPLY

☐ HIS REPLY ☐ HER REPLY

You are about to spend a year abroad and must learn a new language. Describe the steps you would take to accomplish this goal as quickly as possible.

☐ HER REPLY ☐ HIS REPLY

☐ HIS REPLY ☐ HER REPLY

What would you do if you had an unlimited budget to spend?

☐ HER REPLY ☐ HIS REPLY   ☐ HIS REPLY ☐ HER REPLY

If you could only read a certain language, what would that language be?

☐ HER REPLY ☐ HIS REPLY   ☐ HIS REPLY ☐ HER REPLY

What is the best way to be a nice person?

☐ HER REPLY ☐ HIS REPLY

☐ HIS REPLY ☐ HER REPLY

How is it that you feel like you can do anything or that you believe that you can?

☐ HER REPLY ☐ HIS REPLY

☐ HIS REPLY ☐ HER REPLY

Say something about getting stuck into politics

☐ HER REPLY ☐ HIS REPLY

☐ HIS REPLY ☐ HER REPLY

What did you do to get rid of it?

☐ HER REPLY ☐ HIS REPLY

☐ HIS REPLY ☐ HER REPLY

Who made you do it?

☐ HER REPLY ☐ HIS REPLY

☐ HIS REPLY ☐ HER REPLY

Do you get depressed when you look in the mirror? Why? Why not?

☐ HER REPLY ☐ HIS REPLY

☐ HIS REPLY ☐ HER REPLY

List of things that don't have a defined purpose of any kind

☐ HER REPLY ☐ HIS REPLY

☐ HIS REPLY ☐ HER REPLY

What advice would you give to someone who stole something but now feels guilty?

☐ HER REPLY ☐ HIS REPLY

☐ HIS REPLY ☐ HER REPLY

What would you want to learn about your future?

☐ HER REPLY ☐ HIS REPLY

☐ HIS REPLY ☐ HER REPLY

Tell us what you hate?

☐ HER REPLY ☐ HIS REPLY

☐ HIS REPLY ☐ HER REPLY

<h1 style="text-align:center">Write about 2 songs that you love best.</h1>

☐ HER REPLY ☐ HIS REPLY　　　　　　☐ HIS REPLY ☐ HER REPLY

<h1 style="text-align:center">If your parents could see you in a different light, what do you think they'd say?</h1>

☐ HER REPLY ☐ HIS REPLY　　　　　　☐ HIS REPLY ☐ HER REPLY

Would you rather eat the rainbow ice cream or the flower ice cream?

☐ HER REPLY ☐ HIS REPLY   ☐ HIS REPLY ☐ HER REPLY

What's something you don't like about yourself?

☐ HER REPLY ☐ HIS REPLY   ☐ HIS REPLY ☐ HER REPLY

What do your children want when they're learning?

☐ HER REPLY ☐ HIS REPLY

☐ HIS REPLY ☐ HER REPLY

If you could be on any planet, where would it be and why?

☐ HER REPLY ☐ HIS REPLY

☐ HIS REPLY ☐ HER REPLY

☐ HER REPLY ☐ HIS REPLY

☐ HIS REPLY ☐ HER REPLY

☐ HER REPLY ☐ HIS REPLY

☐ HIS REPLY ☐ HER REPLY

How would you describe the feeling of being transported back to an alien world where you are a member of a spacefaring race?

☐ HER REPLY ☐ HIS REPLY   ☐ HIS REPLY ☐ HER REPLY

How would you describe the feeling of being at this stage of your life?

☐ HER REPLY ☐ HIS REPLY   ☐ HIS REPLY ☐ HER REPLY

How would you describe the feeling of being told you cannot do something?

☐ HER REPLY ☐ HIS REPLY

☐ HIS REPLY ☐ HER REPLY

If you could build a car customized just for you, what would it contain?

☐ HER REPLY ☐ HIS REPLY

☐ HIS REPLY ☐ HER REPLY

You have a very special relationship with your dog. Why?

☐ HER REPLY ☐ HIS REPLY   ☐ HIS REPLY ☐ HER REPLY

What do you think makes a good career?

☐ HER REPLY ☐ HIS REPLY   ☐ HIS REPLY ☐ HER REPLY

Describe a memorable experience associated with a particular song or piece of music.

☐ HER REPLY ☐ HIS REPLY

☐ HIS REPLY ☐ HER REPLY

If you could learn any new language, which one would you choose and why?

☐ HER REPLY ☐ HIS REPLY

☐ HIS REPLY ☐ HER REPLY

How would you describe the feeling of being in a uniform after going into the office every day?

☐ HER REPLY ☐ HIS REPLY

☐ HIS REPLY ☐ HER REPLY

Who do you trust the least and why?

☐ HER REPLY ☐ HIS REPLY

☐ HIS REPLY ☐ HER REPLY

How would you describe the feeling of being so healthy?

☐ HER REPLY　☐ HIS REPLY

☐ HIS REPLY　☐ HER REPLY

What's your first reaction when you find a new creature?

☐ HER REPLY　☐ HIS REPLY

☐ HIS REPLY　☐ HER REPLY

List of things that are available

☐ HER REPLY ☐ HIS REPLY

☐ HIS REPLY ☐ HER REPLY

What are you most excited about when working?

☐ HER REPLY ☐ HIS REPLY

☐ HIS REPLY ☐ HER REPLY

Do you stop doing this and that? Why?

☐ HER REPLY ☐ HIS REPLY   ☐ HIS REPLY ☐ HER REPLY

Would you rather keep it a secret or show your true self to the world?

☐ HER REPLY ☐ HIS REPLY   ☐ HIS REPLY ☐ HER REPLY

Write about a time in your life when the content of your character was tested.

☐ HER REPLY ☐ HIS REPLY

☐ HIS REPLY ☐ HER REPLY

How would you describe the feeling that came over you?

☐ HER REPLY ☐ HIS REPLY

☐ HIS REPLY ☐ HER REPLY

What is the most important thing for you right now?

☐ HER REPLY ☐ HIS REPLY

☐ HIS REPLY ☐ HER REPLY

What can I learn from my teacher?

☐ HER REPLY ☐ HIS REPLY

☐ HIS REPLY ☐ HER REPLY

What is the best thing you can do to reduce your dependency on foreign dependencies?

☐ HER REPLY ☐ HIS REPLY

☐ HIS REPLY ☐ HER REPLY

How important is it for you to be happy?

☐ HER REPLY ☐ HIS REPLY

☐ HIS REPLY ☐ HER REPLY

What is one thing you really need to get better at this stage
of your life?

☐ HER REPLY ☐ HIS REPLY   ☐ HIS REPLY ☐ HER REPLY

What is the one thing that you want everyone to be able to do
at any given time?

☐ HER REPLY ☐ HIS REPLY   ☐ HIS REPLY ☐ HER REPLY

Once, when you were very frightened, what happened?

☐ HER REPLY ☐ HIS REPLY

☐ HIS REPLY ☐ HER REPLY

If you could be anywhere, where would it be and why?

☐ HER REPLY ☐ HIS REPLY

☐ HIS REPLY ☐ HER REPLY

If you had to choose one word to describe your unique vision,
which would you use?

☐ HER REPLY ☐ HIS REPLY

☐ HIS REPLY ☐ HER REPLY

What do you seek to eliminate?

☐ HER REPLY ☐ HIS REPLY

☐ HIS REPLY ☐ HER REPLY

Why do you insist on asking about things you've never asked about before?

☐ HER REPLY ☐ HIS REPLY

☐ HIS REPLY ☐ HER REPLY

What is a good reason to lie?

☐ HER REPLY ☐ HIS REPLY

☐ HIS REPLY ☐ HER REPLY

What can you be good for?

☐ HER REPLY ☐ HIS REPLY

☐ HIS REPLY ☐ HER REPLY

What motivates you to give the most of yourself?

☐ HER REPLY ☐ HIS REPLY

☐ HIS REPLY ☐ HER REPLY

How would you describe the feeling of being hypnotized by a stranger?

☐ HER REPLY ☐ HIS REPLY

☐ HIS REPLY ☐ HER REPLY

What do your children think is good or bad?

☐ HER REPLY ☐ HIS REPLY

☐ HIS REPLY ☐ HER REPLY

What has been your greatest accomplishment to date?

☐ HER REPLY ☐ HIS REPLY   ☐ HIS REPLY ☐ HER REPLY

Should you have to take tests in school?

☐ HER REPLY ☐ HIS REPLY   ☐ HIS REPLY ☐ HER REPLY

What would your perfect room look like?

☐ HER REPLY ☐ HIS REPLY   ☐ HIS REPLY ☐ HER REPLY

How would you describe the feeling of being always treated differently?

☐ HER REPLY ☐ HIS REPLY   ☐ HIS REPLY ☐ HER REPLY

Do you do some self-reflection? Does it take time? Why?

☐ HER REPLY ☐ HIS REPLY

☐ HIS REPLY ☐ HER REPLY

Has anything happened that changed you? What's the event?

☐ HER REPLY ☐ HIS REPLY

☐ HIS REPLY ☐ HER REPLY

Would you rather be a woman or a man?

☐ HER REPLY ☐ HIS REPLY

☐ HIS REPLY ☐ HER REPLY

Should there be a dress code in places such as schools, restaurants, and places of business? Why or why not?

☐ HER REPLY ☐ HIS REPLY

☐ HIS REPLY ☐ HER REPLY

How have you been affected by something that someone else did?

☐ HER REPLY ☐ HIS REPLY

☐ HIS REPLY ☐ HER REPLY

Would you rather be a realist and keep living an illusion or become a realist and be the one that has to die?

☐ HER REPLY ☐ HIS REPLY

☐ HIS REPLY ☐ HER REPLY

Say something about something else

☐ HER REPLY ☐ HIS REPLY

☐ HIS REPLY ☐ HER REPLY

List of things that you built in your mind

☐ HER REPLY ☐ HIS REPLY

☐ HIS REPLY ☐ HER REPLY

Would you rather jump from a moving car or a roaring fire?

☐ HER REPLY ☐ HIS REPLY

☐ HIS REPLY ☐ HER REPLY

What is the one thing you regret about your childhood?

☐ HER REPLY ☐ HIS REPLY

☐ HIS REPLY ☐ HER REPLY

If there was a time when you were feeling down before, what kept you going?

☐ HER REPLY   ☐ HIS REPLY   ☐ HIS REPLY   ☐ HER REPLY

List of things that don't go well for you

☐ HER REPLY   ☐ HIS REPLY   ☐ HIS REPLY   ☐ HER REPLY

If you were able to choose one thing from your parents' past that you're most thankful you got to live through, what would it be and why?

☐ HER REPLY ☐ HIS REPLY

☐ HIS REPLY ☐ HER REPLY

How would you describe the feeling of being in a relationship with someone that you know isn't a perfect match?

☐ HER REPLY ☐ HIS REPLY

☐ HIS REPLY ☐ HER REPLY

Is there really a way of getting out of this?

☐ HER REPLY ☐ HIS REPLY

☐ HIS REPLY ☐ HER REPLY

What's your earliest memory of your house?

☐ HER REPLY ☐ HIS REPLY

☐ HIS REPLY ☐ HER REPLY

How would you describe the feeling of being unpopular?

☐ HER REPLY ☐ HIS REPLY

☐ HIS REPLY ☐ HER REPLY

What is most important to you, to be or not to be?

☐ HER REPLY ☐ HIS REPLY

☐ HIS REPLY ☐ HER REPLY

What do you really like about where you live?

☐ HER REPLY ☐ HIS REPLY   ☐ HIS REPLY ☐ HER REPLY

How would you describe the feeling of being a little bit addicted to something? Did you ever wish you could just stop?

☐ HER REPLY ☐ HIS REPLY   ☐ HIS REPLY ☐ HER REPLY

<h1 style="text-align:center">List of your missing things</h1>

☐ HER REPLY ☐ HIS REPLY

____

☐ HIS REPLY ☐ HER REPLY

____

<h1 style="text-align:center">How confident are you?</h1>

☐ HER REPLY ☐ HIS REPLY

____

☐ HIS REPLY ☐ HER REPLY

____

How would you describe the feeling of being watched by an unknown entity?

☐ HER REPLY ☐ HIS REPLY

☐ HIS REPLY ☐ HER REPLY

List of things that you can do to honor someone you lost

☐ HER REPLY ☐ HIS REPLY

☐ HIS REPLY ☐ HER REPLY

Would you like to know something about the author of the
books you are reading? Why?

☐ HER REPLY ☐ HIS REPLY   ☐ HIS REPLY ☐ HER REPLY

If you had to choose one thing in this world that you would
die to protect, that thing would be?

☐ HER REPLY ☐ HIS REPLY   ☐ HIS REPLY ☐ HER REPLY

If you found a treasure worth millions in your backyard, would you keep it a secret or would you tell the world? Why?

☐ HER REPLY ☐ HIS REPLY

☐ HIS REPLY ☐ HER REPLY

How do you make yourself more attractive to men/women?

☐ HER REPLY ☐ HIS REPLY

☐ HIS REPLY ☐ HER REPLY

How would you describe the feeling of being on the cusp of something truly momentous?

☐ HER REPLY ☐ HIS REPLY

☐ HIS REPLY ☐ HER REPLY

List of things that you're looking forward to

☐ HER REPLY ☐ HIS REPLY

☐ HIS REPLY ☐ HER REPLY

What would you do if you were elected president?

☐ HER REPLY ☐ HIS REPLY

☐ HIS REPLY ☐ HER REPLY

What is the strangest wedding you have ever attended?

☐ HER REPLY ☐ HIS REPLY

☐ HIS REPLY ☐ HER REPLY

Tell about one of the most spontaneous and impulsive thing you have ever done.

☐ HER REPLY   ☐ HIS REPLY   ☐ HIS REPLY   ☐ HER REPLY

What did you learn about the human race that you didn't know before?

☐ HER REPLY   ☐ HIS REPLY   ☐ HIS REPLY   ☐ HER REPLY

How do you want to live your life?

☐ HER REPLY ☐ HIS REPLY   ☐ HIS REPLY ☐ HER REPLY

What is your philosophy of life?

☐ HER REPLY ☐ HIS REPLY   ☐ HIS REPLY ☐ HER REPLY

If you suddenly gained the ability to tell whether someone was lying, would you use it?

☐ HER REPLY ☐ HIS REPLY   ☐ HIS REPLY ☐ HER REPLY

Have you ever had a love connection? Tell about it.

☐ HER REPLY ☐ HIS REPLY   ☐ HIS REPLY ☐ HER REPLY

Will you accept you for you? Why?

☐ HER REPLY ☐ HIS REPLY   ☐ HIS REPLY ☐ HER REPLY

What makes people hate you?

☐ HER REPLY ☐ HIS REPLY   ☐ HIS REPLY ☐ HER REPLY

Talk about a time in your life when you experienced nature's indifference to your needs.

☐ HER REPLY ☐ HIS REPLY   ☐ HIS REPLY ☐ HER REPLY

Which is more important to you, to draw strength or learn from life?

☐ HER REPLY ☐ HIS REPLY   ☐ HIS REPLY ☐ HER REPLY

Would you rather travel 100 years into the future or 100 years into the past? Why?

☐ HER REPLY ☐ HIS REPLY

☐ HIS REPLY ☐ HER REPLY

If you could go back in time, what time period would you live in?

☐ HER REPLY ☐ HIS REPLY

☐ HIS REPLY ☐ HER REPLY

What were the most important factors that influenced your decision?

☐ HER REPLY ☐ HIS REPLY

☐ HIS REPLY ☐ HER REPLY

What would you ask for if you could ask for anything in the universe and receive anything in return?

☐ HER REPLY ☐ HIS REPLY

☐ HIS REPLY ☐ HER REPLY

What do you most dislike about yourself?

☐ HER REPLY ☐ HIS REPLY

☐ HIS REPLY ☐ HER REPLY

What kinds of things makes your father happy?

☐ HER REPLY ☐ HIS REPLY

☐ HIS REPLY ☐ HER REPLY

How do you prepare for bedtime?

☐ HER REPLY ☐ HIS REPLY   ☐ HIS REPLY ☐ HER REPLY

How do you deal with the constant pressure of being an idol?

☐ HER REPLY ☐ HIS REPLY   ☐ HIS REPLY ☐ HER REPLY

What is the worst thing that could happen to you?

☐ HER REPLY ☐ HIS REPLY   ☐ HIS REPLY ☐ HER REPLY

What effects does cigarette and alcohol advertising have on young people?

☐ HER REPLY ☐ HIS REPLY   ☐ HIS REPLY ☐ HER REPLY

What's your favorite time of year?

☐ HER REPLY ☐ HIS REPLY

____
____
____
____
____
____
____
____
____

☐ HIS REPLY ☐ HER REPLY

____
____
____
____
____
____
____
____
____

Were there any memorable scenes in your life that made a lasting impression?

☐ HER REPLY ☐ HIS REPLY

____
____
____
____
____
____
____
____

☐ HIS REPLY ☐ HER REPLY

____
____
____
____
____
____
____
____

If you could have only three things in your office or on your desk, what would it be and why?

☐ HER REPLY ☐ HIS REPLY

☐ HIS REPLY ☐ HER REPLY

What was the thing that scared you most as a kid?

☐ HER REPLY ☐ HIS REPLY

☐ HIS REPLY ☐ HER REPLY

What are the most difficult things that have happened in your life?

☐ HER REPLY ☐ HIS REPLY   ☐ HIS REPLY ☐ HER REPLY

Who makes you feel great about being yourself?

☐ HER REPLY ☐ HIS REPLY   ☐ HIS REPLY ☐ HER REPLY

What do your sons need the most in the relationship?

☐ HER REPLY ☐ HIS REPLY

☐ HIS REPLY ☐ HER REPLY

What is the one thing that you regret not doing?

☐ HER REPLY ☐ HIS REPLY

☐ HIS REPLY ☐ HER REPLY

What do you value most in a friendship?

☐ HER REPLY ☐ HIS REPLY   ☐ HIS REPLY ☐ HER REPLY

Do you have organized habits?

☐ HER REPLY ☐ HIS REPLY   ☐ HIS REPLY ☐ HER REPLY

What are the alternatives left that you haven't considered?

☐ HER REPLY ☐ HIS REPLY   ☐ HIS REPLY ☐ HER REPLY

List of things that you want to change.

☐ HER REPLY ☐ HIS REPLY   ☐ HIS REPLY ☐ HER REPLY

What's your favorite moment in your entire life?

☐ HER REPLY ☐ HIS REPLY

____

☐ HIS REPLY ☐ HER REPLY

____

What can you do to combat climate change today?

☐ HER REPLY ☐ HIS REPLY

____

☐ HIS REPLY ☐ HER REPLY

____

Would you rather just leave it and move on?

☐ HER REPLY ☐ HIS REPLY

☐ HIS REPLY ☐ HER REPLY

Say something about what you do that's important

☐ HER REPLY ☐ HIS REPLY

☐ HIS REPLY ☐ HER REPLY

Do you respect everyone? Why?

☐ HER REPLY ☐ HIS REPLY

☐ HIS REPLY ☐ HER REPLY

If you had to choose one thing that could make people more like themselves, what would it be?

☐ HER REPLY ☐ HIS REPLY

☐ HIS REPLY ☐ HER REPLY

If you found a magic lamp what 3 wishes would you ask the Genie for? What would each mean to you?

☐ HER REPLY ☐ HIS REPLY   ☐ HIS REPLY ☐ HER REPLY

What is the best thing you remember doing?

☐ HER REPLY ☐ HIS REPLY   ☐ HIS REPLY ☐ HER REPLY

How do you deal with grief?

☐ HER REPLY ☐ HIS REPLY   ☐ HIS REPLY ☐ HER REPLY

Why do you think they did this to us?

☐ HER REPLY ☐ HIS REPLY   ☐ HIS REPLY ☐ HER REPLY

Do you enjoy reading? Why?

☐ HER REPLY ☐ HIS REPLY   ☐ HIS REPLY ☐ HER REPLY

How do you know what is real and what isn't?

☐ HER REPLY ☐ HIS REPLY   ☐ HIS REPLY ☐ HER REPLY

☐ HER REPLY ☐ HIS REPLY

☐ HIS REPLY ☐ HER REPLY

☐ HER REPLY ☐ HIS REPLY

☐ HIS REPLY ☐ HER REPLY

What is the best thing about a movie that you have never seen?

☐ HER REPLY   ☐ HIS REPLY

☐ HIS REPLY   ☐ HER REPLY

Is there anything you want to get rid of in your life?

☐ HER REPLY   ☐ HIS REPLY

☐ HIS REPLY   ☐ HER REPLY

Do you have good habits? Tell me about it.

☐ HER REPLY   ☐ HIS REPLY   ☐ HIS REPLY   ☐ HER REPLY

How do you feel about being a target of hate and negativity?

☐ HER REPLY   ☐ HIS REPLY   ☐ HIS REPLY   ☐ HER REPLY

If you had to choose one thing that is important about your life, what would it be?

☐ HER REPLY ☐ HIS REPLY

☐ HIS REPLY ☐ HER REPLY

How would you describe the feeling of a family?

☐ HER REPLY ☐ HIS REPLY

☐ HIS REPLY ☐ HER REPLY

If you had to choose one thing to be the most important lesson I've learned along the way, what would it be?

☐ HER REPLY ☐ HIS REPLY   ☐ HIS REPLY ☐ HER REPLY

What do you believe to be a normal state of being?

☐ HER REPLY ☐ HIS REPLY   ☐ HIS REPLY ☐ HER REPLY